Congressional
Research
Service

Employment for Veterans: Trends and Programs

Benjamin Collins, Coordinator
Analyst in Labor Policy

David H. Bradley
Specialist in Labor Economics

Cassandria Dortch
Analyst in Education Policy

Lawrence Kapp
Specialist in Military Manpower Policy

Christine Scott
Specialist in Social Policy

October 23, 2012

Congressional Research Service

7-5700

www.crs.gov

R42790

CRS Report for Congress ———————————————
Prepared for Members and Committees of Congress

Summary

Veterans' employment outcomes in the civilian labor market are an issue of ongoing congressional interest. This report offers introductory data on veterans' performance in the civilian labor market as well as a discussion of veteran-targeted federal programs that provide employment-related benefits and services.

According to federal data, the unemployment rate for veterans who served after September 2001 is higher than the unemployment rate for nonveterans. Conversely, the unemployment rate for veterans from prior service periods (a much larger population than post-9/11 veterans) is lower than the nonveteran unemployment rate. The varied demographic factors of each of these populations likely contribute to these variations, though their degree of influence is unclear.

There are a number of federal programs to assist veterans in developing job skills and securing civilian employment. Broadly speaking, these programs can be divided into (1) general veterans' programs, (2) programs that target veterans with service-connected disabilities, and (3) competitive grant programs that offer supplemental services but may be limited in scope.

General veterans' programs begin with transition programs that are provided to exiting members of the Armed Forces. These transition programs cover a variety of topics including information on identifying occupations that align with military skills and specializations, conducting job searches, applying for employment, and navigating veterans' benefits. One of the most common veterans' benefits is educational funding through the GI Bill. The GI Bill programs typically provide funding for education or training programs as well as housing allowance while the veteran is enrolled. Veterans who are no longer eligible for the GI Bill may receive training benefits through the newly created Veterans Retraining Assistance Program (VRAP).

Veterans who are seeking employment without obtaining additional training may receive job search assistance and other services from Local Veterans Employment Representatives (LVER). Veterans who wish to pursue employment in the federal government are assisted by several policies that give them preference in the competitive hiring process or, in some cases, allow them to forego the competitive process and be appointed directly.

Veterans with service-connected disabilities who have obstacles to employment may be assisted by the Vocational Rehabilitation and Employment (VR&E) program. This program provides assistance in identifying an occupation that is consistent with the veterans' skills and interests and providing the services (including educational services) necessary to achieve that outcome. Disabled veterans can also receive assistance from the Disabled Veterans Outreach Program (DVOP), which provides assistance in local labor markets.

In addition to these nationwide programs, the federal government also funds competitive grant programs for state, local, and private entities to provide employment-oriented services to veterans. These include the Veterans Workforce Investment Program (VWIP), which may provide training or employment services and Veterans Upward Bound (VUB), which prepares educationally disadvantaged veterans for postsecondary coursework.

Contents

Figures

Tables

Contacts

Background

Veterans' employment outcomes in the civilian sector are an issue of ongoing congressional interest that has received particular attention during the current period of relatively high unemployment. A number of programs currently exist to assist veterans in obtaining or training for civilian employment. There is regular congressional debate about expanding or otherwise amending these programs to better serve veterans.

This report discusses veterans' employment trends and programs. The first section presents data on veterans' employment outcomes, identifying recent trends, and discussing issues to consider when interpreting veterans' employment data. The following sections present brief discussions of existing programs that provide employment-related services to veterans. These services are divided into (1) general programs that are broadly available to veterans, (2) programs that target veterans with service-connected disabilities, and (3) competitive grant programs that provide additional employment-related services to veterans but may be limited in scope or availability.

Notably, this report does not attempt to provide an exhaustive list of all programs that may assist veterans in the labor market nor does it attempt to provide comprehensive information on the programs is discusses. Instead, it aims to provide a broad overview of the largest employment-related programs as well as some more recent initiatives that may inform future policy. For detailed information on each program, readers are encouraged to refer to the CRS reports or other sources that are referenced in each section.[1]

Employment Trends Among Veterans[2]

Estimates of veterans' employment and unemployment are published by the Bureau of Labor Statistics (BLS). The estimates are derived from the Current Population Survey (CPS), a monthly household survey in which respondents may self-identify as veterans. Veterans' employment outcomes are frequently compared to the employment outcomes for nonveterans to establish veterans' relative performance in the labor market.

This section will divide workers into three groups: (1) Gulf War II veterans who served at any point after September 2001, (2) veterans from prior service periods, and (3) nonveterans.[3] Since these populations vary in many characteristics that may influence employment outcomes, comparisons between these groups should be conducted with caution.

Recent employment outcomes for veterans and non-veterans are presented in **Table 1**.[4] As the table shows, the unemployment rate for Gulf War II (GWII) veterans is higher than the

---

[1] References also include a CRS analyst to contact about the topic. In cases where a topic does not list a contact, inquiries should be directed to the coordinator of this report.

[2] This section was prepared by Benjamin Collins, Analyst in Labor Policy, bcollins@crs.loc.gov, 7-7382.

[3] The designation Gulf War II veterans follows the definition set by the Bureau of Labor Statistics. Data for veterans from other periods were calculated by subtracting GWII data from total veterans data.

[4] In **Table 1** and **Figure 1**, CRS calculated quarterly estimates by aggregating monthly data to control for large month-to-month fluctuations.

unemployment rates of both veterans from other periods of service as well as nonveterans. GWII veterans, however, constitute less than 20% of the veteran labor force (about 2 million of just under 11 million).

Table 1. Employment Outcomes by Veteran Status, Third Quarter 2012

	Population (thousands)	Labor Force (thousands)	Unemployed (thousands)	Unemployment Rate
All Veterans	21,132	10,972	736	6.7%
Gulf War II Veterans	2,524	2,039	201	9.9%
Other Veterans	18,609	8,933	535	6.0%
Nonveterans	213,584	142,352	11,259	7.9%

Source: Quarterly data calculated by CRS based on monthly data from the Bureau of Labor Statistics' Employment Situation historical data for Table A-5, generated at http://www.bls.gov/webapps/legacy/cpsatab5.htm.

Notes: Sum of veterans groups may not equal veterans total due to rounding. Gulf War II veterans are those who served any time after September 2001. Nonveterans exclude persons under age 18. Data are not seasonally adjusted; seasonally adjusted estimates are not available.

Several factors that are not observable in **Table 1** should also be considered when interpreting the employment data in the table.[5]

- *The GWII veteran labor force is younger than the nonveteran labor force.* About 63% of GWII veterans in the labor force are under the age of 35, compared to about 37% of nonveterans in the labor force. Since younger workers generally have higher unemployment rates than older workers, GWII veterans' relative youth may influence their unemployment rate.[6]

- *Veterans have a different educational distribution than nonveterans.* Among those in the labor force, only 1% of GWII veterans and 3% of other veterans have less than a high school education, compared to 9% of nonveterans. Conversely, the proportion of college graduates among the labor forces of GWII veterans (31%) and other veterans (30%) are somewhat lower than nonveterans (36%).[7] The effect of this different educational distribution on veterans' employment outcomes is unclear.

- *Disability issues.* In 2011, approximately 14% of all veterans and 26% of GWII veterans reported a service-connected disability. While service-connected disabilities do appear to be related to lower rates of labor force participation and

---

[5] Data on veterans' characteristics are 2011 annual averages and from Bureau of Labor Statistics, "Employment Situation of Veterans—2011," March 20, 2012, http://www.bls.gov/news.release/vet.htm. Monthly data on veterans' characteristics are not published by BLS.

[6] Ibid. Table 2A.

[7] Ibid. Table 3. Data only consider veterans age 25 and over. About 11% of the GWII veterans in the labor force are under the age of 25.

higher rates of unemployment among labor force participants, the differences in employment outcomes between disabled and non-disabled veterans are modest. Among veterans of all service periods, the labor force participation rate for veterans with a service-connected disability was slightly lower than for veterans without a service-connected disability (49% v. 52%) and the unemployment rate was slightly higher (8.5% v. 7.9%). When limited to GWII veterans, the difference in participation rate is similar (80% v. 84%) and difference in unemployment rate (12.1% and 9.5%) is somewhat larger.[8] Comparable data on employment outcomes for nonveterans with disabilities are not available.

- *Categorization of post-military transition period.* Recent veterans who have not yet secured post-service employment are categorized as unemployed and entitled to unemployment insurance. The classification of this transition period may increase GWII veterans' unemployment rate.

Figure 1 presents recent historical data on unemployment rates for GWII veterans, other veterans, and nonveterans.[9] Several trends emerge over the 16-quarter reference period:

- *The unemployment rate for GWII veterans is very dynamic.*[10] This is likely due to their relatively small sample size in the CPS. Short-term trends for this population (such as the spike in the unemployment rate in mid-2010 and the large drop in the unemployment rate at the beginning on 2012) should be interpreted with caution.

- *The unemployment rate for GWII veterans is typically above that of other veterans and nonveterans.* The 16-quarter average unemployment rate was 10.7% among GWII veterans, 7.4% among other veterans, and 8.7% among nonveterans. Quarterly data are not available prior to the fourth quarter of 2008. Annual data from 2005 to 2008, however, are similar to recent trends with unemployment rates for GWII veterans that are higher than those of nonveterans and unemployment rates of other veterans that are lower than those of nonveterans.[11]

- *The unemployment rate for each group trends similarly over the reference period.* While the dynamic nature of the GWII veterans' unemployment rate somewhat masks this trend, each group's unemployment rate followed a generally upward trend from late 2008 to early 2010 and then a downward trend in the subsequent quarters. The similarity of these trends underscores the influence of the broader labor market on veterans' employment outcomes.

---

[8] Ibid. Table 6. Data that cross-tabulates period of service, disability status, and employment status are not available. Approximately 17% of veterans did not report their disability status.

[9] The reference period was determined by the earliest availability of monthly data for GWII veterans.

[10] While aggregating monthly data into quarterly totals somewhat reduces the dynamism of these estimates, the unemployment rate for GWII veterans still fluctuates more than larger populations.

[11] 2005 was the first year that BLS published data on GWII veterans. Data are available from "The Employment Situation of Veterans" press releases from BLS, archived at http://www.bls.gov/schedule/archives/all_nr.htm#VET. "The Employment Situation of Veterans" has been an annual release in 2007. Prior to 2007, it was issued on a biennial basis.

Figure 1. Unemployment Rates by Veteran Status, 2008-2012

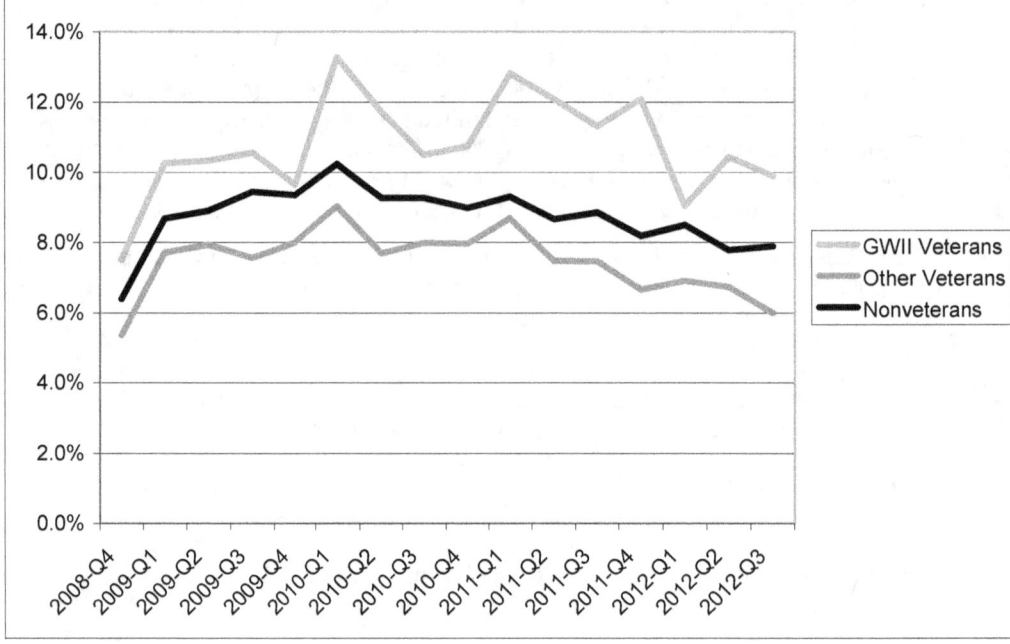

Source: Quarterly data calculated by CRS based on monthly data from the Bureau of Labor Statistics' Employment Situation historical data for Table A-5, generated at http://www.bls.gov/webapps/legacy/cpsatab5.htm.

Notes: Gulf War II veterans are those who served any time after September 2001. Nonveterans excludes persons under age 18. Data are not seasonally adjusted so quarter-to-quarter comparisons should be conducted with caution. Seasonally adjusted estimates for veterans' employment are not available.

Current Employment-Related Programs for Veterans

This report highlights the primary training and employment services programs that are available to veterans. It does not, however, attempt to present a comprehensive list of employment-related programs for veterans. This report emphasizes programs available to veterans of active duty and generally omits discussion of programs that target former members of the military reserve. It also omits discussions of programs or program components that provide benefits to eligible family members of veterans.

The veteran-targeted programs in this report are presented in **Table 2**. Each is discussed in greater detail in the subsequent text. These programs are grouped into three categories:

- *Programs that are broadly available to veterans.* While they may have some eligibility limitations, these programs are generally available to veterans with or without a service-connected disability;

- *Programs that are available to veterans with service-connected disabilities.* These programs include the Vocational Rehabilitation and Employment program as well specialized versions of some generally available veterans programs; and

- *Competitive grant programs.* These programs fund employment-related services for veterans but may be limited in scope or local availability.

This report does not discuss the Small Business Administration programs for veterans that provide entrepreneurial support and loan guarantees.[12]

Table 2. Employment-Related Programs, Benefits, and Services for Veterans

Program	Description	FY2012 Funding
General Programs, Benefits, and Services for Veterans		
Transition Assistance Program (TAP) / Transition Goals Plans Success (Transition GPS)	TAP provides services to exiting service members related to obtaining civilian employment and otherwise transitioning to civilian life. Transition GPS is currently in the process of replacing TAP. Transition GPS will be a mandatory program for nearly all exiting service members with expanded services over a five-day curriculum.	$9 million appropriation from Department of Labor (DOL); $50 million from the Department of Defense (DOD)[a]
Educational Benefits (GI Bill)	GI Bill programs generally provide funds for educational costs as well as living expenses while enrolled in educational programs. The most-used program for recent veterans is the Post-9/11 GI Bill.	$10.5 billion[b]
Veterans Retraining Assistance Program (VRAP)	VRAP provides educational benefits for unemployed veterans between the ages of 35 and 60 who are not eligible for a GI Bill or other Department of Veterans Affairs (VA) educational program. VRAP benefits are limited to 12 months.	$197 million[c]
Local Veterans Employment Representatives (LVER)	LVER funds state personnel positions that assist veterans in securing employment in their local area. LVER activities include but are not limited to outreach to local employers and referral to training or education benefits. LVER is funded out of Jobs for Veterans State Grant (JVSG) funds.	$165 million appropriation from DOL (also funds DVOP)
Federal Hiring Preferences and Special Hiring Authorities	Veterans receive preference when applying for nearly all competitively-hired federal employment. There are also special hiring authorities in which qualified veterans may be directly appointed to a position that would otherwise be competitively hired.	not applicable
Work Opportunity Tax Credit (WOTC)	Employers who hire veterans who meet various criteria (such as long-term unemployment or receipt of benefits under the Supplemental Nutrition Assistance Program) are eligible for a tax credit equal to a portion of the veteran's wages.	estimates limited to veterans provisions not available
Priority of Service in DOL training programs	Veterans receive priority of service for any DOL-funded training or employment service program that they are eligible for as a member of the general public.	not applicable

[12] For information on these programs, see CRS Report R42695, *SBA Veterans Assistance Programs: An Analysis of Contemporary Issues*, by Robert Jay Dilger and Sean Lowry.

Program	Description	FY2012 Funding
Programs for Veterans with Service-Connected Disabilities		
Vocational Rehabilitation and Employment (VR&E)	VR&E provides counseling to assist veterans with service-connected disabilities to identify an employment objective and support and/or training services to fulfill that objective.	$ 949 million[d]
Disabled Veterans Outreach Program (DVOP)	DVOP funds state personnel positions that provide intensive employment services to disabled and other high-need veterans.	$165 million appropriation from DOL (also funds LVER)
Specialized versions of other programs	TAP, Federal hiring preference, and WOTC all have specialized components that target veterans with service-connected disabilities.	Included in general program costs
Competitive Grant Programs that Provide Supplemental Services		
Veterans Workforce Investment Program	VWIP provides competitive grants to public and nonprofit organizations to provide training and/or employment services to veterans.	$14.6 million appropriation from DOL
Collaborative Veterans' Training, Mentoring, and Placement Program	This program provides funds to nonprofit agencies to provide employment-related services to veterans.	$4.5 million appropriation from the VA for two-year program
Veterans Upward Bound (VUB)	VUB provides services such as tutoring and application assistance to aid veterans in preparing for a program of postsecondary education	$13 million appropriation from the Department of Education (ED)

Source: Sources are listed in each program's section of this report.

a.   DOD has estimated that its FY2013 costs will increase to $200 million due to the implementation of Transition GPS.

b.   Program is an entitlement not subject to appropriations. FY2012 costs are estimates for Post-9/11 GI Bill and Montgomery GI Bill-Active Duty only and do not include administrative expenses.

c.   Estimated expenditures for FY2012. The program did not begin until July 1, 2012, so the estimate in the table reflects partial-year expenditures. Estimated expenditures for FY2013, when the program will run the entire fiscal year, are $1.1 billion.

d.   Program is an entitlement and not subject to appropriation. FY2012 costs are estimates and include benefits and subsistence allowances; they do not include administrative and counseling expenses.

General Veterans' Employment and Training Programs

The programs discussed in this section are available to most veterans of active duty. In the interest of simplicity, this report generally does not present detailed eligibility criteria for each program and benefit, though it does attempt to note eligibility requirements that categorically exclude large numbers of veterans (such as the eligibility window following discharge for GI Bill benefits). This report may omit requirements that would exclude relatively few veterans, such as most programs' exclusion of veterans who were dishonorably discharged.[13] The specific eligibility criteria for each program will usually be available in the external sources that are referenced in the report section that discusses the program.

Transition Programs for Separating Members of the Armed Forces[14]

In 1990, as the post-Cold War drawdown was beginning, Congress authorized a set of benefits and services to assist military personnel in the transition to civilian life.[15] Some of these authorities continued in effect after the drawdown was complete and formed the basis of the Transition Assistance Program (TAP). TAP is currently undergoing substantial modification. A pilot program, Transition Goals Plans Success (Transition GPS), is underway and is expected to completely replace TAP by the end of 2013.[16] Both programs are described below.

Transition Assistance Program (TAP)

TAP provides pre-separation services and counseling on a number of transition-related topics to separating members of the Armed Forces. In addition to guidance on broader transition issues such as financial management and health care, TAP includes information on the following employment issues as they relate to veterans:

- the correlation between military skills and civilian occupations;

- professional certifications, including licensing and apprenticeships;

- public and community service opportunities, including federal employment opportunities and veterans' hiring preferences (described in a subsequent section of this report);

- self-employment and entrepreneurship, including veterans' small business and entrepreneurship programs; and

- education and training assistance, including use of veterans' educational benefits and other job training opportunities.

Separating personnel can also elect to participate in a three-day employment workshop, which covers skills such as choosing a career, conducting job searches, interviewing, and writing cover letters and resumes, as well as providing analyses of employment conditions in various occupations and the labor market at large. Separating personnel can also opt to attend a four hour veterans' benefits brief sponsored by the VA.

A Disabled Transition Assistance Program (DTAP) also exists within TAP. In addition to the above mentioned services, DTAP includes individual instruction for disabled service members regarding their job-readiness and special needs they might have as a result of their disability,

---

[13] For a more detailed discussion factors that may influence a former service member's eligibility for veterans' benefits, see CRS Report R42324, *"Who is a Veteran?"—Basic Eligibility for Veterans' Benefits*, by Christine Scott.

[14] This section written by Lawrence Kapp, Specialist in Military Manpower Policy (x7-7609) and Fenwick Gilroy, Research Associate.

[15] Codified at 10 U.S.C. 1141-1150.

[16] Terri Cronk, "New Program Aims to Better Help Troops Transition to Civilian Life," American Forces Press Service, August 18, 2012, available at http://www.defnese.gov/news/newsarticle.aspx?id=117544.

along with information on the VA's Vocational Rehabilitation and Employment services (described later in this report).

TAP services are provided at many military installations, often found in the military installation's career or family support offices. The Department of Defense (DOD), Department of Labor (DOL), Department of Veterans Affairs (VA), and the Department of Homeland Security (DHS) are each involved in conducting TAP.[17]

Transition GPS

Transition GPS is the name of the redesigned transition assistance program brought about by the work of the executive branch's Veterans' Employment Initiative Task Force and intended to conform with the Veterans Opportunity to Work (VOW) to Hire Heroes Act of 2011.[18] Among other changes, the VOW Act made participation in TAP mandatory for nearly all separating military personnel and required that each TAP participant receive "an individualized assessment of the various positions of civilian employment in the private sector for which such member may be qualified" as a result of their military training. These statutory changes take effect on November 21, 2012, one year after the enactment of the VOW Act.

DOD introduced the Transition GPS pilot program at seven military bases in the summer of 2012. It includes a five-day core program that incorporates the elements of TAP described above into a redesigned curriculum. Some of the key differences between TAP and Transition GPS include

- the five-day core curriculum is mandatory, not optional, for nearly all separating servicemembers;

- class sizes will be smaller to provide individual attention;

- the individual transition plan is standardized, tied to the servicemembers personal goals, and includes a "skills-gap" analysis;

- successful completion is based on achieving "career readiness standards," not simply attendance;

- the program concludes with a "capstone event" to verify that career readiness standards have been achieved; and

- in addition to the core curriculum, servicemembers will be able to participate in optional tracks for education, entrepreneurship, and technical training.

In order to comply with the deadline set by the VOW Act, DOD expects the "core" Transition GPS curriculum to be in place by November 21, 2012. The optional tracks are expected to be implemented by the end of 2013.

---

[17] Memorandum of Understanding between the Department of Labor, Department of Defense, Department of Veterans Affairs, and Department of Homeland Security, "Transition Assistance Program and Disabled Transition Assistance Program," signed September 19, 2006, available at http://www.dol.gov/vets/vpls/VPL%20Attachments/VPL%201-08%20Attch%201%20-%20Transition%20Assistance%20and%20Disabled%20Transition%20Assistance%20Programs%20Memorandum%20of%20Understanding%20dated%20September%2019,%202007.pdf.

[18] The VOW to Hire Heroes Act is Title II of P.L. 112-56. In addition to modifying TAP, the law had other provisions related to veterans' employment. The VOW to Hire Heroes Act will be referred to as "the VOW Act" throughout this report.

GI Bill Educational Assistance Programs[19]

The VA administers several educational assistance programs for veterans (commonly known as GI Bills) that are intended to avert unemployment, adjust veterans to civilian life, reward military service, encourage recruitment and retention in the military, and make education affordable. VA educational assistance payments are available for approved programs of education as well as living expenses while enrolled.[20]

While there are several GI Bill programs, the vast majority of veterans who utilize education benefits do so under the Post-9/11 GI Bill[21] or the Montgomery GI Bill-Active Duty (MGIB-AD). Both programs provide benefits for 36 months of full-time schooling or the equivalent in part-time attendance.[22] The Post-9/11 GI Bill provides separate payments for tuition, fees, supplies, and housing. The maximum benefit for tuition and fees at a public educational institution is equal to in-state tuition and fees for that institution. As of August 1, 2012, the maximum benefit for tuition and fees at a private or foreign institution is $18,078 per academic year. The monthly housing allowance under the Post-9/11 GI Bill varies by geographical location and ranges from $765 in the Mansfield, Ohio area to $2,835 in the New York City area.[23] MGIB-AD provides a single monthly payment to the veteran to cover both education and living expenses. As of October 1, 2012, the maximum benefit under MGIB-AD is $1,564 per month.

Post 9/11 GI Bill benefits are typically available within 15 years of discharge or release from active duty. MGIB-AD benefits (and most other GI Bill benefits) are generally available within ten years. Notably, GI Bill benefits are not considered when calculating a student's eligibility for need-based Pell grants, meaning that a veteran who meets Pell grant criteria may receive both Pell grants and GI Bill benefits.[24] As an additional benefit, educational assistance received under a VA education program (including subsistence or housing allowances for enrolled veterans) is not subject to federal income tax.

In its FY2013 budget, the VA estimated that in total FY2012 benefits for the Post-9/11 GI Bill and Montgomery GI Bill-Active Duty were $10.5 billion.[25]

---

[19] For more information on each of the GI Bills, including the statutory authorization of each program, see CRS Report R40723, *Educational Assistance Programs Administered by the U.S. Department of Veterans Affairs*, by Cassandria Dortch.

[20] Eligible educational programs include but are not limited to college courses, vocational programs, entrepreneurship courses, apprenticeships, on-the-job training, and licensing or certification tests.

[21] The Post-9/11 GI Bill is formally known as the Post-9/11 Veterans Educational Assistance Program. For more information, see CRS Report R42755, *The Post-9/11 Veterans Educational Assistance Act of 2008 (Post-9/11 GI Bill): Primer and Issues*, by Cassandria Dortch.

[22] Benefits can be used in nonconsecutive months. For example, a veteran may use GI Bill benefits for four traditional nine-month full-time academic years.

[23] Monthly housing allowances under the Post-9/11 GI Bill equal the monthly basic allowance for housing for a member of the Armed Forces with dependents in pay grade E-5 in the military housing area in which the veteran's educational institution is located. Local rates are available at http://www.defensetravel.dod.mil/Docs/perdiem/browse/Allowances/BAH/PDF/2012/2012-With-Dependents-BAH-Rates.pdf.

[24] For more information on Pell Grants, see CRS Report R42446, *Federal Pell Grant Program of the Higher Education Act: How the Program Works, Recent Legislative Changes, and Current Issues*, by Shannon M. Mahan.

[25] The FY2013 budget was issued in February 2012. See Volume III of the FY2013 VA Budget, page 2B-2 at http://www.va.gov/budget/docs/summary/Fy2013_Volume_III-Benefits_Burial_Dept_Admin.pdf.

Veterans Retraining Assistance Program (VRAP)[26]

The VRAP program was created by the VOW Act to provide employment-related training for older unemployed veterans who were no longer eligible for the GI Bill.[27] It provides up to 12 months of training benefits to unemployed veterans who are not eligible for other VA education programs and are between the ages of 35 and 60.[28] It is administered by the VA.

VRAP benefits are limited to training at community colleges or technical schools in occupations that DOL has identified as "high demand."[29] Monthly benefit levels are limited to the maximum amounts under the MGIB-AD program (described in the "Programs" section above). While benefits are limited to 12 months, veterans may enroll in programs longer than 12 months. In cases where a program is less than 12 months, benefits are limited to the duration of the program.

VRAP is limited to 45,000 participants from July 1, 2012 to September 30, 2012 and 54,000 participants from October 1, 2012 to March 31, 2014. The VA has estimated that in FY2013, the first full year of the program, VRAP obligations will be $1.1 billion.[30]

Local Veterans Employment Representatives (LVER) Employment Services[31]

The LVER program provides formula grants to states to hire personnel that provide assistance to veterans who are seeking employment.[32] LVER staff provide employment services to veterans and conduct outreach to local employers to develop employment opportunities for veterans. Outreach activities might include advocacy efforts to local employers and workshops for veterans seeking employment. LVER staff are familiar with a range of veteran services and may provide referral to other entities in the support of veterans seeking employment.

Statute specifies that, "to the maximum extent possible," states should hire veterans as LVER personnel, with the highest preference is given to veterans with service-connected disabilities who are otherwise qualified for the position.[33] LVER personnel work in conjunction with the One-Stop delivery system, and are often physically stationed at One-Stop Career Centers, as established by the Workforce Investment Act of 1998 (WIA; P.L. 105-220).[34]

---

[26] For more information on the VRAP program, including current application procedures and current enrollment levels, see http://benefits.va.gov/vow/education.htm.

[27] VRAP was created by Section 211 of P.L. 112-56.

[28] Veterans are ineligible for VRAP if they received a dishonorable discharge, are receiving VA compensation due to unemployability, or are enrolled in a federal or state job training program.

[29] The VA has identified more than 200 occupations as eligible for VRAP benefits. See http://benefits.va.gov/vow/docs/VRAP_High_Demand.pdf for the complete list.

[30] See Volume III of the FY2013 VA Budget, page 2B-2 at http://www.va.gov/budget/docs/summary/Fy2013_Volume_III-Benefits_Burial_Dept_Admin.pdf.

[31] This section was prepared by David H. Bradley, Specialist in Labor Economics, dbradley@crs.loc.gov, 7-7352.

[32] LVER is codified at 38 U.S.C. 4104.

[33] See 38 U.S.C. 4104(c).

[34] For more information on WIA and One-Stop Career Centers, see CRS Report R41135, *The Workforce Investment Act and the One-Stop Delivery System*, by David H. Bradley.

The LVER program is part of the Jobs for Veterans State Grant (JVSG) program, which is administered by the Veterans Employment and Training Service (VETS) of DOL.[35] JVSG also provides funds for the Disabled Veterans Outreach Program (DVOP), which is described in a subsequent section of this report. In FY2012, JVSG's budget authority was approximately $165 million. JVSG is funded out of the Employment Security Administration Account in the Unemployment Trust Fund.

Priority of Service in DOL-Funded Training and Employment Service Programs

In addition to veteran-targeted programs, DOL administers a number of public programs to assist individuals in training for and securing employment. These services include subsidized training as well as employment services such as job search assistance and resume preparation. The Jobs for Veterans Act of 2002 (P.L. 107-288) specifies that veterans will receive priority of service in all DOL-funded training programs.[36] DOL has clarified that this includes all services provided at One-Stop Career Centers (including employment services such as job search assistance).[37]

In 2011, DOL launched a Gold Card initiative directed at Post-9/11 veterans. In addition to priority in all training programs, the initiative also provides veterans with intensive employment services such as job readiness assessments, career guidance, and referral to training through WIA, an apprenticeship, or other federal or state programs. Veterans may also receive six months of follow-up services from a case manager.[38]

Skills and Experience Transfer

While there are no appropriated programs that exclusively support the transfer of military skills to the civilian labor market, there are several tools that can assist veterans and service providers (such as TAP administrators and LVER personnel) in identifying occupations that utilize military skills and experience. Examples of these tools include the VA's Military Skills Translator[39] and O*Net's MyNextMove for Veterans[40] (funded by DOL). The National Resource Directory, a veterans-directed collaboration between the Department of Defense (DOD), DOL, and the VA, also has a skills translator that is connected to localized employment listings.[41]

The VOW Act addresses the issue of transferring military skills with a demonstration project that requires DOL to select five military occupational specialties with skills that are transferrable to high-growth civilian industries. DOL then must work with a coalition of federal, state, and private

---

[35] More information on veteran-related initiatives administered the U.S. Department of Labor, including the JVSG program, is available at http://www.dol.gov/vets/.

[36] To receive priority of service, a veteran must meet the program's eligibility criteria regarding age, employment history, or other characteristics.

[37] See 20 C.F.R. 1010.200-330.

[38] More information on the Gold Card initiative is available at http://www.dol.gov/vets/goldcard.html.

[39] See https://mst.vaforvets.va.gov/mst/va/mos-translator.

[40] See http://www.mynextmove.org/vets/.

[41] See https://www.nrd.gov/home/veterans_job_bank.

entities to determine what military skills, training, and experience may align with requirements for civilian credentials, certifications, and licenses.[42]

Another law enacted in the 112th Congress related to transferring military experience into civilian credentials. In July 2012, the president signed the Veteran Skills to Jobs Act (P.L. 112-147). The law states that "The Head of each Federal licensing authority shall consider and may accept, in the case of any individual applying for a license, any relevant training received by such individual while serving as a member of the armed forces[.]"

Veterans may also be able to convert their military training, skills, and experience into postsecondary education credit if they enroll in a school that participates in the Servicemembers Opportunity College (SOC) consortium.[43] Institutions in the SOC Consortium agree to adhere to a set of servicemember-focused policies. Among these is the consideration of converting military experience and training into postsecondary credit.

Work Opportunity Tax Credit (WOTC) for Employers[44]

The WOTC provides a tax credit for employers who hire qualified veterans. In cases where the eligible hire works at least 400 hours, the credit is equal to 40% of the wages paid to the eligible veteran, up to a certain level.[45] The VOW Act established the current credit amounts and veteran criteria:

- a maximum credit of $2,400 for hiring a veteran who is receiving Supplemental Nutrition Assistance Program (SNAP; formerly food stamps) benefits for at least three months during the year prior to hire;

- a maximum credit of $2,400 for hiring a veteran who has been unemployed for a total of a least four weeks but less than six months in the year prior to hire;

- a maximum credit of $4,800 for hiring a veteran who is eligible for disability compensation from the VA and is within one year of discharge or release from military duty;

- a maximum credit of $5,600 for hiring a veteran who has been unemployed for a total of at least six months in the year prior to hire; and

- a maximum credit of $9,600 for hiring a veteran who is eligible for disability compensation from the VA and who has been unemployed for a total of six months in the year prior to hire.

---

[42] See P.L. 112-56, Section 237 and 38 U.S.C. 4114.

[43] The SOC consortium is privately administered. For more information on the Consortium, see http://www.soc.aascu.org/.

[44] For more information on the WOTC, see CRS Report RL30089, *The Work Opportunity Tax Credit (WOTC)*, by Christine Scott. This report also describes nonveteran populations that were eligible for the WOTC under prior law.

[45] The size of the WOTC is based on wages paid the employee during the first year of employment. In cases where an eligible hire works between 120 and 400 hours, the tax credit is reduced to 25% of wages paid. If the eligible hire works fewer than 120 hours, the employer is not eligible for the credit.

The WOTC was previously available to employers that hired individuals in other target populations (e.g., at-risk youth or convicted felons). Under current law, only the veterans groups described above are eligible for the WOTC. The WOTC is set to expire on December 31, 2012.

Federal Employment[46]

There are several programs and policies that provide a preference for veterans in obtaining employment in the federal government. These policies and programs can either give veterans an advantage in the competitive hiring process or, in some cases, allow a veteran to be appointed without going through the competitive process.

Points Preference

In the federal hiring process for competitive positions, candidates may be evaluated through a system that assigns point values to relevant experience, skills, and education. Depending on the specifics of their active military service, veterans may receive extra points added to their numerical score.

A five-point preference is available to veterans who served after September 11, 2001.[47] A five point-preference is also available to veterans who served during specified wartimes or in specified campaigns.[48] A ten-point preference is available to veterans who either (1) have a service-connected disability or (2) received a Purple Heart. The ten-point preference is available to these veterans regardless of their period or location of service.

Special Hiring Authorities

There are several hiring programs that allow qualified veterans to be appointed to what would otherwise be competitive federal positions without having to compete with the general public. Typically, these programs allow an agency to hire a veteran in a shorter period of time than it would take to fill the position through the competitive service process. To be eligible for these special hiring authorities, a veteran must be have been separated from the Armed Forces for less than three years, have served in a qualified combat mission, or be disabled.[49]

Other Initiatives

In 2009, President Barack Obama issued Executive Order 13518, which aimed to "enhance recruitment of and promote employment opportunities for veterans within the executive branch[.]"[50] The program established a Council on Veterans Employment that included 24

---

[46] For a more in-depth discussion of federal employment for veterans, see CRS Report RS22666, *Veterans Benefits: Federal Employment Assistance*, by Christine Scott.

[47] The service period under this criteria is set to end on the date prescribed by Presidential proclamation or law as the last date of Operation Iraqi Freedom. As of this writing, no such proclamation or law has been issued.

[48] Applicable dates and criteria are available from the Office of Personnel Management at http://www.opm.gov/staffingportal/vetguide.asp#2When.

[49] Full details on these hiring authorities is available from the Office of Personnel Management at http://www.opm.gov/staffingportal/vetguide.asp#6.

[50] The full text of the order, including a list of participating agencies, is available at http://www.gpo.gov/fdsys/pkg/FR-
(continued...)

agencies and required each agency to develop an agency-specific plan and designate an office or officer for promoting employment opportunities for veterans within the agency. The order also established a website that offered veteran-specific information on obtaining federal employment as well as contact information for the individual or office in each agency responsible for promoting veterans' employment within the agency.[51]

The VOW Act expanded on this effort by directing the Office of Personnel Management (OPM) to (1) designate agencies to establish a program to provide employment assistance to separating service members and (2) ensure that those programs are coordinated with the Transition Assistance Program for existing service members (discussed later in this report).

Programs for Veterans with Service-Connected Disabilities

Dedicated employment services exist for veterans with service-connected disabilities. The Vocational Rehabilitation and Employment (VR&E) program provides comprehensive services for veterans with a service-connected disability and does not have an analogue among general veterans' program.[52] Other programs for disabled veterans are specialized variations of general programs that were discussed previously.

Vocational Rehabilitation and Employment (VR&E)[53]

VR&E provides job training and employment services to veterans who have service-connected disabilities.[54] To be entitled to VR&E services, a veteran with a service-connected disability must also demonstrate an employment handicap that hinders the veteran's ability to prepare for, obtain, or retain employment consistent with his or her abilities, aptitudes, and interests.

VR&E offers several tracks of services, depending on the veteran's employment objective and needs. Veterans who already have the necessary job skills or seek to return to previous employment can receive short-term services such as resume assistance and job accommodations. Veterans who need job skills are eligible for education and training benefits as well as employment services once they complete training. The VA has reported that long-term services, including training, is the most-utilized VR&E track.

In FY2012, VR&E benefits are estimated to be approximately $949 million. Program administration, including counseling, are estimated to be an additional $204 million.[55]

(...continued)

2009-11-13/pdf/E9-27441.pdf.

[51] See http://www.fedshirevets.gov/AgencyDirectory/index.aspx for a list of agency contacts.

[52] Veterans who participate in the VR&E program may not participate in the GI Bill.

[53] For more information on the VR&E program, see CRS Report RL34627, *Veterans' Benefits: The Vocational Rehabilitation and Employment Program*, by Benjamin Collins.

[54] VR&E also provides independent living services to veterans who are not able to work. In FY2011, approximately 25% of completed rehabilitations under VR&E were independent living (i.e., not employment-based) rehabilitations.

[55] See Volume III of the FY2012 VA budget at http://www.va.gov/budget/docs/summary/Fy2013_Volume_III-Benefits_Burial_Dept_Admin.pdf.

Disabled Veterans Outreach Program (DVOP) Employment Services[56]

DVOP provides formula grants to states to hire staff to provide a range of intensive services to veterans with service-connected disabilities as well as other veterans with multiple barriers to employment.[57] Services include case management, referral to other service providers (e.g., the VA's VR&E program discussed in the prior subsection), employment counseling, and job search assistance.

DVOP is part of DOL's JVSG program, which also funds the previously discussed LVER program.[58] In FY2012, JVSG's budget authority was approximately $165 million. JVSG is funded out of the Employment Security Administration Account in the Unemployment Trust Fund.

Components of General Programs that Target Disabled Veterans

Several of the broader veterans programs described previously in this report, have specialized components for disabled veterans. Additional detail can be found in the sources referenced in each program's primary section of this report.

- *Transition Assistance Program.* The Disabled Transition Assistance Program (DTAP), provides specialized services for exiting service members with service-connected disabilities.

- *Federal Employment.* As discussed in the section above, veterans with a service-connected disability are eligible for the highest preference in competitively-hired federal positions. Disabled veterans are also eligible for special hiring authorities, including noncompetitive appointments for qualified veterans with a disability rating of 30% or more from the VA.[59]

- *Work Opportunity Tax Credit.* Some WOTCs are available for businesses that hire veterans who are eligible for disability compensation from the VA. The largest available tax credit is for hiring a veteran who is eligible for disability compensation and who was unemployed for at least 6 of the 12 months prior to hire.

Veteran-Targeted Competitive Grant Programs

Additional programs provide competitive grants for entities that provide services to veterans. Since the programs are competitive grants, they may only be available in certain areas, may have limited capacity, or may only serve a targeted veteran population.

---

[56] This section was prepared by David H. Bradley, Specialist in Labor Economics, dbradley@crs.loc.gov, 7-7352.

[57] DVOP is codified at 38 U.S.C. 4103A.

[58] JVSG is described in greater detail in the "Local Veterans Employment Representatives (LVER) Employment Services" section of this report. More information on veteran-related initiatives administered the U.S. Department of Labor, including the JVSG program, is available at http://www.dol.gov/vets/.

[59] For more information on the "30% or More Disabled Veterans" hiring authority, see http://www.opm.gov/staffingportal/vetguide.asp#30%Disabled.

The programs discussed below do not include competitive grant programs that include employment services as part of a broader group of services. For example, the employment components of the Homeless Veterans Reintegration Program are omitted.[60]

TRIO Veterans Upward Bound (VUB)[61]

The TRIO Veterans Upward Bound (VUB) program provides services to assist veterans in preparing for a program of postsecondary education. VUB projects provide academic instruction, tutoring, assistance in completing secondary school, assistance with college admissions and applications, and assistance applying for financial assistance. It is administered by the Department of Education (ED).

To be eligible for participation, veterans must be in need of academic support to pursue education beyond secondary school successfully. At least two-thirds of program participants must be low-income, potential first-generation college students. The remaining one-third of participants must be either low-income, potential first generation college students, or otherwise be at-risk of academic failure. The program defines a veteran who is at-risk for academic failure as an individual who has been out of high school or dropped out of a program of postsecondary education for five or more years; has scored on standardized tests below the level that demonstrates a likelihood of success in a program of postsecondary education; or meets the definition of an individual with a disability.

In 2012, appropriations for VUB were $13 million.[62]

Veterans Workforce Investment Program (VWIP)[63]

WIA authorizes grants for programs to meet the needs of "veterans with service-connected disabilities, veterans who have significant barriers to employment, veterans who served on active duty in the Armed Forces during a war or in a campaign or expedition for which a campaign badge has been authorized, and recently separated veterans." Programs may contain training or other employment services.

In FY2012, $14.6 million was appropriated for these grants. A 2012 Solicitation for Grant Applications expressed an intention of awarding grants ranging from $750,000 to $1,250,000 for a three-year period of performance.[64]

---

[60] The Homeless Veterans Reintegration Program is discussed in CRS Report RL34024, *Veterans and Homelessness*, by Libby Perl.

[61] For more information on TRIO programs, including Upward Bound, see CRS Report R42724, *The TRIO Programs: A Primer*, by Cassandria Dortch.

[62] See Department of Education FY2012 Budget, Higher Education, Higher Education Section, page S-125 at http://www2.ed.gov/about/overview/budget/budget13/justifications/s-highered.pdf.

[63] VWIP is authorized by Section 168 of WIA. Questions on VWIP should be directed to David H. Bradley, dbradley@crs.loc.gov, 7-7352.

[64] See for more information on VWIP, including the PY2012 SGA, see http://www.dol.gov/vets/programs/vwip/main.htm.

Collaborative Veterans' Training, Mentoring, and Placement Program

The VOW Act requires the VA to award grants to nonprofit agencies to "to provide training and mentoring for eligible veterans who seek employment." Grant recipients are required to collaborate with local DVOP personnel as well as state and local workforce agencies to "facilitate the placement of the veterans that complete the training in meaningful employment that leads to economic self-sufficiency."[65]

This program is smaller than the other competitive grant programs discussed in this section. The VOW Act authorizes a total of $4.5 million to carry out this activity in FY2012 and FY2013. The VOW Act specifies that grants will go to no more than three organizations.

Author Contact Information

Benjamin Collins, Coordinator
Analyst in Labor Policy
bcollins@crs.loc.gov, 7-7662

David H. Bradley
Specialist in Labor Economics
dbradley@crs.loc.gov, 7-7352

Cassandria Dortch
Analyst in Education Policy
cdortch@crs.loc.gov, 7-0376

Lawrence Kapp
Specialist in Military Manpower Policy
lkapp@crs.loc.gov, 7-7609

Christine Scott
Specialist in Social Policy
cscott@crs.loc.gov, 7-7366

---

[65] See Section 234 of P.L. 112-56.